CW00456867

Wildflowers
of
Coastal
Northumberland

Wendy Dickson

Photographs
by Wendy Dickson

Keepdate Publishing

Published by Keepdate Publishing Ltd.
21 Portland Terrace, Jesmond
Newcastle upon Tyne NE2 1QQ, UK.
Telephone (0191) 2819444

© Wendy Dickson
© Photographs by Wendy Dickson
© 2000 Keepdate Publishing Ltd.

ISBN 1 899506 36 5

Apart from any fair dealing for the purposes of research or private study, or criticism or review, as permitted under the Copyright, Design and Patents Act 1988, this publication may not be reproduced, stored or transmitted, in any form or by any means, without the prior permission in writing of the publishers, or in the case of reprographic reproduction in accordance with the terms of licences issued by the Copyright Licensing Agency. Inquiries concerning reproduction outside those terms should be sent to the publishers at the address above.

Designed and typeset by
Keepdate Publishing Ltd, Newcastle upon Tyne

foreword

Northumberland has beautiful coastal scenery and a rich coastal flora. Wendy Dickson has lived and worked in Northumberland over a number of years and was so attracted by the flowers she saw that she set about photographing them. This is her selection of photographs, all taken in Northumberland, and each with both the English and scientific name of the plant. I am sure that residents, visitors and tourists alike will find this not just an attractive book but also a useful one for identifying plants which can be seen growing along the coast.

Professor George Swan

introduction

The Northumberland coast is richly endowed with scenery – much of it designated Heritage Coastline and an Area of Outstanding Natural Beauty. One of the pleasures of walking the coastline in summer is the abundance of wildlife and particularly the richness of flowering plants.

The inspiration for this book came from several sources. Firstly, taking regular walks along the coastline inspired me to start photographing some of the flowers I saw. Then a book of flower photographs was published in my second home of Shetland, which gave me the idea to gather together my own pictures and do something about them. Finally I was fortunate enough to go on a coastal walk under the auspices of the Natural History Society of Northumbria, led by Professor George Swan. I learnt a lot on this walk from the county's most eminent botanist.

In 1993 the *Flora of Northumberland* was published, again under the auspices of the Natural History Society of Northumberland with Professor Swan as its author. This botanists' 'bible' will remain the standard work for Northumberland's plants well into the new century.

This small book is intended as a photographic celebration of some of Northumberland's coastal flora. The logical sequence follows the order of plants in the aforementioned tome which itself is based mainly on the *Flora Europaea* with one or two exceptions.

Acutely conscious of my own botanical shortcomings, I had long been aware that I needed to get my pictorial identifications checked by an experienced botanist, but never dreamt that would be none other than Professor Swan himself. Without his generosity of time and good–natured approach to the task, as well as contributing the Foreword, this publication would probably never have seen the light of day. I am greatly indebted to Professor Swan and any errors remaining are entirely of my own making.

Each picture caption gives both the 'popular' and scientific name of the plant, together with a note of the month and location in which it was photographed, followed by a few lines of commentary. I hope that every reader, resident or visitor, will get as much pleasure out of looking at the photographs as I did out of taking them, and that – if you haven't already – it will inspire you to go out and have a look for yourself at some of the floral delights of this northernmost part of England's coastline.

Last, but by no means least, I would like to express my thanks to Keepdate Publishing for their friendly help and guidance through the production stages of this book.

Wendy Dickson

Maidenhair Spleenwort
Asplenium trichomanes
Bamburgh, May.

Although not a flowering plant, the delicate leaves of this fern brighten up walls and rocks across a wide part of Northumberland.

Creeping Willow
Salix repens
Holy Island, May.

A number of willow species grow in the county, most of them probably native like this low–growing one which, as its name implies, creeps along the ground.

Amphibious Bistort
Persicaria amphibia
Druridge Bay Country Park, July.

This plant has two forms: a smaller one that grows on land and this one whose hairless and long–stalked leaves float on the water surface forming an excellent backdrop for the lovely pink flowers.

Sea–purslane
Atriplex portulacoides
Alnmouth, July.

Although not a common habitat on the Northumberland coast, wherever saltmarsh occurs, so Sea Purslane grows. Its tiny yellow flowers are far less conspicuous than the grey–green colour of the leaves, caused by tiny papery scales filled with air.

Sea Sandwort
Honckenya peploides
Alnmouth, May.

This bold little plant with its inconspicuous white flowers is a great coastal dune stabiliser for its shiny, fleshy leaves can carpet areas of shifting sand. As the sand builds around it, so it grows upwards, spawning new mini–dunes.

Sea Mouse–ear
Cerastium diffusum
Near Craster, May.

This is a very localised plant of the coast. The mouse–ear family is said to derive its name from the shape and hairiness of its leaves, resembling the ears of the rodent.

Lesser Sea–spurrey
Spergularia marina
Long Nanny, June.

Another charming plant of the dunes, this one merits a closer look. Nowadays it can also be found colonising road verges where winter salting has taken place.

Ragged–Robin
Lychnis
flos–cuculi
Craster, July.

Although widespread in suitable damp grassland, this plant with its 'ragged' pink flowers is becoming an increasingly rare sight in Northumberland.

Sea Campion
Silene uniflora
Farnes, June.

Although essentially a coastal plant, it formerly grew at one inland site in the Cheviots. Similar to the taller Bladder Campion, it has broader petals with fewer flowers per cluster, interspersed with non–flowering shoots.

Red Campion
Silene dioica
Alnmouth, May.

This plant may well be familiar, as it is widespread throughout the county. The flower colour varies considerably from red right through to pale pink, the latter sometimes the result of the plant hybridising with the white–flowered Bladder Campion.

Bulbous Buttercup
Ranunculus bulbosus
Alnmouth, May.

A widespread native of Northumberland, this, the main buttercup of limestone, is one of the earliest to flower. Its name derives from the stem's swollen base while the bent–back sepals beneath the petals are a good identification clue.

Celery–leaved Buttercup
Ranunculus sceleratus
Low Newton, June.

This very poisonous member of the buttercup family is mainly a coastal plant, occurring in muddy patches of water, even where this is brackish.

Lesser Meadow–rue
Thalictrum minus
Boulmer, June.

The flowers of this delightful plant tremble in the breeze. In Northumberland it is mainly confined to the coast where the most common of several forms can be found on sand dunes and crags of whinstone.

Common Poppy
Papaver rhoeas
Holy Island, June.

Poppies are unashamed colonists, but few would complain of the presence of these showy plants.

Common Fumitory
Fumaria officinalis
Boulmer, July.

The name fumitory is said to come from a Latin word literally meaning 'smoke of the earth', apparently because the roots, when pulled up, give off a smell akin to nitric acid. In America it is known as 'fume root'.

Hedge Mustard
Sisymbrium officinale
Boulmer, June.

As the name suggests, this plant has a piquant taste. At one time it was mixed with honey as a cure for asthma. Its tall spiky countenance can be seen in a variety of habitats.

9

Wallflower
Erysimum cheiri
Bamburgh, May.

Thought to have originally come from Greece, the wallflowers that grace the dunes at Bamburgh probably escaped from cultivated plants, but nonetheless add a splash of colour among the marram grass.

Cuckooflower
Cardamine pratensis
Druridge Bay Country
Park, May.

There are two
explanations for the
name of this abundant
plant of damp places:
that it flowers at the
time cuckoos start to
be heard, and that it
frequently gets covered
in 'cuckoo spit', the
frothy substance that
tiny insects called
froghoppers create to
protect their young.

Scurvy Grass
Cochlearia
officinalis **agg.**
Dunstanburgh, May.

Contrary to its name,
this group of
microspecies
belongs to the
cabbage family. Rich
in Vitamin C, our
forefathers used it to
prevent scurvy, a
killer disease
common in the days
of long sailing
voyages when diets
were poor.

Sea Rocket
Cakile maritima
Newton Links, July.

Very much a coastal plant, usually growing at
the top of the beach where its flowers, which
may be pink, mauve or white, and its fleshy
foliage often form a distinct line above the
highest strandline along this hostile habitat.

Wild Mignonette
Reseda lutea
St Mary's Island,
June.

This plant is a colonist, and can be found on areas of disturbed ground. The name Mignonette is derived from the French 'mignon' which means cute or delicate.

Biting Stonecrop
Sedum acre
Holy Island, June.

This native plant is also known as Wall–pepper from the fiery taste of its fleshy leaves. In the past it has been used medicinally for curing all manner of complaints; planting it on roofs was also said to prevent thunderstorms.

White Stonecrop
Sedum album
Holy Island, July.

Another member of the stonecrop family, this white–flowered species is not a native in this country. As well as growing on rocky places including walls, it also occurs on sand–dunes.

Meadow Saxifrage
Saxifraga granulata
Craster, May.

Several species of this striking family grow in the county most of which, like this one, are native, while a few are garden escapes. Meadow Saxifrage can be found not only on whin grassland on parts of the coast but also right across the county.

Grass–of–Parnassus
Parnassia palustris
Holy Island, August.

Despite its name, this is
not a grass but in a
family of its own. Said to
be named after Mount
Parnassus, sacred to the
god Apollo, each stem
holds up a white flower
whose five petals are
delicately traced in
green.

Meadowsweet
Filipendula ulmaria
Holy Island, July.

Meadowsweet is strongly
scented. Originally known
as medesweet, due to being
used as a flavouring for
mead, how appropriate
that today this widespread
plant grows well on Holy
Island, where mead is still
produced.

Burnet Rose
Rosa pimpinellifolia
Newton Links, June.

Burnet Rose is very much a plant of coastal sand dunes, and is well protected by an awesome array of distinctively straight thorns and stiff bristles.

Salad Burnet
Sanguisorba minor
subsp. *minor*
Newton Links,
June.

This insignificant
looking plant has
separate male,
female and bisexual
flowers. The tiny
leaves have long
been used in salads,
offering a hint of
the smell of
cucumber.

Pirri–pirri–bur
*Acaena
novae–zelandiae*
Holy Island, June.

Almost certainly
accidentally
introduced with wool
imported from
Australia in the early
1900s, this plant's
armoury of efficient
hooks mat together
to adhere to clothes,
fur and feather, often
with fatal results. It
should be treated
with the utmost
respect to prevent it
spreading further.

Silverweed
Potentilla anserina
Howick, July.

As its name suggests, this member of the rose family
is regarded by many as a weed whose long runners
help it to spread. It is the underside colour of the
leaves that give the plant its name.

Creeping Cinquefoil
Potentilla reptans
Bamburgh, July.

It is not hard to see
how cinquefoils get
their name, the very
distinctive leaves being
divided into five parts.
Within the family,
hybridisation is not
infrequent.

Hawthorn
Crataegus monogyna
Holy Island, May.

A native and naturalised plant of Northumberland, hawthorn is familiar both as a major constituent of hedges and as part of the scrub community. On the coast it grows among dunes where bushes provide cover and songposts for small birds.

Gorse
Ulex europaeus
Craster, May.

Gorse must be one of the most familiar plants, especially when its golden flowers give off their heady aroma. The more prominent of two species in the county, this and Western Gorse hybridise from time to time.

Tufted Vetch
Vicia cracca
Druridge Bay
Country Park,
July.

Conspicuous
because of its
bright
purplish–blue
flowers, this is a
common and
familiar plant of
grassland and
hedgerows.

Purple Milk–vetch
Astragalus danicus
Newton Links, June.

A lover of limestone, this
plant occurs among the
short turf of mature sand
dunes and whinstone which
hug the coastline.

Bush Vetch
Vicia sepium
Boulmer, June.

The scientific name for vetches,
Vicia, comes from Latin *vincio*
meaning to bind, referring to the
tendrils which are a feature of the
vetches, vetchlings and peas,
distinguishing them from other
members of the pea family.

Meadow Vetchling
Lathyrus pratensis
Boulmer, June.

This is one of the plants that fixes nitrogen through its roots and thus enriches the soil. It is a widespread flower of the coast.

Common Restharrow
Ononis repens
Newton Links, July.

A member of the pea family, the deep roots of this plant used to severely impede – or resist – the line of the harrow, hence its name. Occasionally plants bearing white flowers can be found among the more usual pink ones of the dunes.

24

Lesser Trefoil
Trifolium dubium
Craster, May.

A very common, native plant of Northumberland, found on areas of short grassland on well–drained soils. One of a small group of very similar species, when the petals drop from this plant they reveal straight brown seedpods.

Red Clover
Trifolium pratense
Beadnell, June.

A well–known member of a very familiar family, this is a grassland plant. Another nitrogen fixer, it is popular with farmers whose ground it helps to fertilise; a past use was to relieve whooping cough.

Common Bird's–foot–trefoil
Lotus corniculatus
Cullernose, May and Newton Links, July.

One of the food plants of the Common Blue Butterfly, this familiar plant has over 70 folknames throughout the country. Trefoil refers to its leaf arrangement and bird's foot to the shape of the seedpod.

Kidney Vetch
Anthyllis vulneraria
Hauxley, May.

This native plant can be found in a variety of habitats from sand dunes and cliff tops to roadside verges. Known as a herb that helps heal wounds, the kidney–shaped flowers also led to the belief that it could cure kidney disease.

Bloody Crane's–bill
Geranium sanguineum
Newton Links, July.

One of the most impressive sights on our dunes in summer is the flowering of Bloody Cranesbill. Get in close and you will see how delicately–veined the flowers are. 'Bloody' comes from the leaves changing to blood red as the season progresses.

Dove's–foot Crane's–bill
Geranium molle
Newton Links, May.

Crane's–bills get their name from the shape of the seedhead resembling the bill of a crane. This widespread but unimposing member of the family's additional likeness to a dove's foot comes from the shape of its leaves.

Cut–leaved Crane's–bill
Geranium dissectum
Druridge Pools, June.

Again the leaf shape marks out this species from others in the family. It is a taller, more sprawling plant than the previous one and occurs frequently in grassy areas and on waste ground.

Common Stork's–bill
Erodium cicutarium
Newton Links, July.

A plant of sand dunes, it is common on the coast though not confined to it. The seedhead is corkscrew shaped which, when ripe, helps it to burrow down where it lands. Individual flowers may only last half a day; once pollinated they fall.

Common Mallow
Malva sylvestris
Holy Island, June.

Mallow is an imposing plant with its bush–like growth and numerous pink flowers. The naturalist Pliny is said to have used mallow sap diluted with water to prevent aches and pains.

Slender St. John's–wort
Hypericum pulchrum
Craster, July.

Said to be named after St. John the Baptist, in some parts of the country people used to gather this plant on the eve of St. John's Day to protect them from evil spirits. This is one of several members of the family occurring in Northumberland.

Common Dog–violet
Viola riviniana
Dunstanburgh, May.

This violet is unscented and was thus thought to be inferior to the scented varieties – fit only for dogs. The beautifully marked petals more than compensate for this and serve to attract insects visually instead.

Common Rock–rose
Helianthemum nummularium
Craster, May.

Common Rock–rose, the only member of its family growing in Northumberland, is scattered across the northern and south–western parts of the county, occurring on underlying limestone, whinstone and other igneous rocks.

Rosebay Willowherb
Chamerion angustifolium
Holy Island, July.

Although a native, it is only since the First World War that this plant spread across Northumberland. Today it brightens up many a patch of waste ground and is foodplant to caterpillars of some of the hawkmoths.

Great Willowherb
Epilobium hirsutum
Alnmouth, July.

This less brash relative of Rosebay Willowherb prefers damper areas, where it can spread vegetatively beneath the soil. It is pollinated mainly by hoverflies and bees, and is a foodplant for the caterpillars of the elephant hawkmoth.

Alexanders
Smyrnium olusatrum
Tynemouth, April.

The Romans were responsible for bringing this striking yellow–flowered umbellifer to this country from the Mediterranean. Its name refers to Alexander the Great of Macedonia, where it is used as a pot herb.

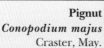

Pignut
Conopodium majus
Craster, May.

The edible tubers of this member of the carrot family were dug out by pigs trained to smell them in the same way they do truffles on the continent. It is a widespread plant of grassy areas.

Hemlock
Conium maculatum
Low Newton, June.

While some umbellifers have widespread culinary uses, this plant is highly poisonous. Its purple–blotched stem and unpleasant smell help identify it.

Hogweed
Heracluem sphondylium subsp.
sphondylium
Boulmer, June.

Unfortunately considered by many to be a pernicious weed, this plant is much loved by insects, particularly hoverflies and soldier beetles. As its name implies, it has also been used in the past as pig fodder.

Primrose
Primula vulgaris
Cocklawburn Dunes,
April.

As with the Cowslip, with which it sometimes hybridises, the primrose produces two kinds of flower – pin–eyed and thrum–eyed, to prevent self–pollination. *Primula*, from the Latin *Primus*, means one of the first to flower.

Cowslip
Primula veris
Newton Links, May.

Legend tells that the first cowslip sprang up at the spot where the keys of Heaven fell when St. Peter dropped them after discovering a duplicate set existed. Nowadays, cowslips occur along much of the Northumbrian coastline and may be increasing.

Sea–milkwort
Glaux maritima
Newton Links, June.

This tiny plant that occurs in saltmarsh areas along the coast has no petals – instead the pale pink sepals form the flowers. To compensate for the salty habitat, it stores water in its fleshy leaves.

Bog Pimpernel
Anagallis tenella
Holy Island, July.

The delicate pink flowers of this low–growing plant shun shade, preferring to open in sunshine and close in dull weather. A lover of damp areas, it is becoming scarcer throughout Britain due to drainage and cultivation.

Scarlet Pimpernel
Anagallis arvensis
subsp. *arvensis*
Holy Island, June.

Perhaps better known from the novel named after it, this small plant occurs in sand dunes along the coast, but is also a plant of cultivation, including gardens. Its tiny scarlet flowers could well be overlooked.

Thrift
Armeria maritima
subsp. *maritima*
Cullernose Point, May.

This plant, whose pink flowers are common all along our coast, featured on the old threepenny piece in the mistaken understanding of its name which, in fact, derives from its thriving, or remaining green, right through the year.

Common Sea–lavender
Limonium vulgare
St. Cuthbert's Island, July.

The name belies the rarity of this native
Northumberland plant, which is confined to
only one site in the county – St. Cuthbert's
Island off the south–west corner of Holy Island.

Seaside Centaury
Centaurium littorale
subsp. *littorale*
Holy Island, July.

The first British record for this plant was in Northumberland. A plant of sand dunes, dune slacks and damp sea cliffs, today it is scarce and localised here at the southern limit of its distribution on the east coast of Britain.

Autumn Gentian
Gentianella amarella
subsp. *amarella*
Newton Links, August.

Just when most plants are nearing the end of their flowering period, autumn gentians add their subtle colours – dark mauves though sometimes almost white – to grassland and coastal dunes. It has been credited with numerous medicinal properties.

Lady's Bedstraw
Galium verum
Boulmer, July.

When Lady's Bedstraw is in flower on the dunes, the prolific clusters of tiny yellow flowers are hard to miss. Although typically a dune plant, it also occurs inland.

Crosswort
Cruciata laevipes
Newton Links, June.

A close relative of the bedstraws, this plant flowers earlier and is much less typically coastal, being widespread throughout the county. The small flowers have four yellow petals diagonally opposite, forming a cross.

Sea Bindweed
Calystegia soldanella
Druridge Bay, July.

This plant, with its distinctive kidney-shaped leaves, was only found in the county in 1973, and is now known from only four sites, with only one locality further north on the east coast of Britain.

Field Bindweed
Convolvulus arvensis
Craster, July.

What a pity this pretty plant is no friend of the gardener. As it grows, so it wraps itself around other plants in a stranglehold, and that fact, along with its deep and extensive root system, makes it difficult to eradicate.

Viper's–bugloss
Echium vulgare
Holy Island, July.

This splendidly
showy plant with
its pink buds
turning to blue
flowers is a lover
of dry sandy
ground, dunes
and sea cliffs. In
Northumberland
it is fairly local but
also grows inland
in a few locations.

Comfrey
Symphytum sp.
St. Mary's Island,
June.

Comfrey has a history of use by herbalists. Its roots were packed round broken limbs, it was used to draw out splinters, and made into a drink to relieve back pains. It has also been used as a vegetable.

Green Alkanet
Pentaglottis
sempervirens
Alnmouth, May.

Not a native of
Britain, it is
uncertain when this
plant was
introduced and why.
Northumberland
clearly suits it for it
is said to have
spread greatly in the
county during the
present century.

Scarce Fiddleneck
Amsinckia lycopsoides
Farne Islands, June.

This North American
plant is thought to have
been introduced to its
only Northumberland
location on Inner
Farne Island by a
lighthouse keeper
distributing his chicken
feed. Arctic Terns nest
among the
orange–yellow flowers.

Changing Forget–me–not
Myosotis discolor
Craster, June.

The flowers of this plant change colour
during the course of their short lives –
opening as creamy white or yellow and then
turning blue as they mature: hence its name.

Hound's–tongue
Cynoglossum officinale
Newton Links, June.

The small maroon flowers can easily be
overlooked but deserve more attention.
Mainly confined to the coast but with a
few inland locations, much folklore is
attached to Hound's–tongue and it has
been exploited for various medicinal
properties. This is a rather pale
specimen.

Wood Sage
Teucrium scorodonia
Craster, July.

With a name like this it may seem an unlikely plant of the coast, but it is frequent and widespread throughout the county in a variety of habitats.

White Dead–nettle
Lamium album
Alnmouth, May.

Considered a weed by many, a closer look will reveal how beautifully marked the white petals are in order to attract pollinating insects. Although the harmless leaves resemble stinging nettle, it is in a completely different family.

Marsh Woundwort
Stachys palustris
Holy Island, August.

Marsh Woundwort has a history of use as a healing herb with its foliage being applied as a poultice to wounds. The young shoots have also been used cooked and eaten in a similar manner to asparagus.

Wild Thyme
Thymus polytrichus subsp. *britannicus*
Craster, July.

Immortalised by Oberon in Shakespeare's A Midsummer Night's Dream – "I know a bank whereon the wild thyme grows...", this plant occurs from sea–level to the hills, and graces many an area with its mat of mauve flowers.

Henbane
Hyoscyamus niger
Holy Island, July.

Highly poisonous, containing
alkaloids with hallucinogenic and
analgesic properties, this striking plant
bears large creamy yellow flowers
delicately veined in mauve, and gives
off an unpleasant odour. If you
 encounter it – look but don't touch.

Common Toadflax
Linaria vulgaris
Alnmouth, July.

Coastal sand dunes are just one of a number
of habitats in which this relative of the
snapdragons might be found. The flower
shape is such that only heavy insects such as
bumblebees can gain entry to the nectar
and thus pollinate the flowers.

Ivy–leaved Toadflax
Cymbalaria muralis
Holy Island, August.

This relative of Common Toadflax is
much more diminutive, and favours
walls and rocks, though it will not
always respond to artificial help in new
sites. A native of southern Europe, it
greatly increased in Northumberland
during the 19th century.

Foxglove
Digitalis purpurea
Craster, July.

A poisonous plant, it is much more likely to be encountered in woodland glades than on the coast, but is widespread throughout the county. The majority of flowers are a deep pink to purple shade – though white ones are not uncommon.

Germander Speedwell
Veronica chamaedrys
Holy Island, May.

A number of different speedwells grow in the county of which this species is, perhaps, one of the more familiar, and by no means confined to the coast.

Eyebright
Euphrasia agg.
Newton Links, June.

The name eyebright covers a group of species and hybrids that are all but impossible to separate in the field. Eyebright grows prolifically among sand dunes and short turf along many parts of the coast.

Red Bartsia
Odontites vernus
Holy Island, June.

A small, rather undistinguished–looking plant, with mauvish–pink rather than red flowers, it is semi–parasitic on grasses, from whose roots it obtains water and minerals. Although quite widely spread, it is not common in the county.

Yellow–rattle
Rhinanthus minor
Druridge Pools, June.

Another plant semi–parasitic on grasses, it is, however, far more plentiful than the previous species, particularly in pasture land. The name rattle refers to the seeds which, when ripe, rattle around inside the seed capsule before release.

**Buck's–horn
Plantain**
Plantago coronopus
Newbiggin, June.

This attractive plant
can very easily be
overlooked for some
specimens are very
small. The
distinctive leaves,
likened to the horns
or antlers of a deer,
grow in a rosette
and the coast is its
preferred habitat.

Hoary Plantain
Plantago media
Newton Links, August.

This plantain is the odd one out in
the family for while the others are
pollinated by wind, this has a faint
scent to attract pollinating insects.
It is also a major indicator species
of underlying limestone.

Red Valerian
Centranthus ruber
Holy Island, June.

This striking plant brightens up the walls
and castles of Holy Island and Bamburgh
with its showy reddish–pink flowers, some
even white, the colour ranging from plant
to plant. It was introduced to Britain from
the Mediterranean.

Small Scabious
Scabiosa columbaria
Low Stead, July.

The links south of Howick are a kaleidoscope of colour in July and this plant is one of the contributors. The scabious family is so named because the juice was once used to cure scabies and other unpleasant skin diseases.

Harebell
Campanula rotundifolia
Boulmer, July.

Confusingly, this plant is known as Scottish Bluebell across the border. With its nodding blue flowers, it likes grassy links and dunes. As the fruit capsules develop, it becomes more upright to enable breezes to carry off the seeds.

Hemp–agrimony
Eupatorium cannabinum
Cullernose, July.

Growing up to three feet in height, this plant occurs in a variety
of habitats from sea cliffs and riverbanks to damp woodlands
and roadside verges. Its clusters of tiny pink flowers give way to
seedheads with parachutes of white hairs to aid dispersal.

Daisy
Bellis perennis
Newbiggin, June.

Can there be a more
despised flower than
this amazing survivor?
Yet a closer look at
the Daisy, prized by
Chaucer and likened
to earthbound stars by
Shelley, will reveal its
resemblance to a
small sun – hence
'day's eye'!

Sea Aster
Aster tripolium
Alnmouth, July.

Almost entirely a plant of the coast and tidal stretches of rivers, it has more recently been found along roadside verges whose saline content has risen from road–salting. Its previous garden popularity was usurped by the larger Michaelmas Daisy.

Yarrow
Achillea millefolium
Boulmer, July.

Flowering in colours from white through pink to pale mauve, this very common plant has deep roots that help it survive cutting machines. In the past it has been used to cure several ailments and was also said to increase physical attractiveness.

Tansy
Tanacetum vulgare
Boulmer, August.

Rub your hand against a leaf of Tansy and you will at once discover its strongly aromatic properties. Its strong flavour is probably the reason why its use in cooking has died out; its medicinal properties have been legendary.

Colt's–foot
Tussilago farfara
Hauxley, May.

Colt's–foot can easily confuse the unwary, for rarely, as in this picture, do you see the flowers, one of the earliest to appear in spring, and the hoof–shaped leaves, which appear later, together.

Common Ragwort
Senecio jacobaea
Alnmouth, July.

Considered in many places to be an agricultural pest plant which is poisonous to livestock, it is the foodplant of the caterpillars of the handsome cinnabar moth that can show off their bright yellow and black warning colouration as they are protected by ingesting the alkaloid poisons contained in the leaves which birds find distasteful.

Carline Thistle
Carlina vulgaris
Bamburgh, July.

Not common in the county, the yellow–brown flowers which open in dry weather and close when it is damp – making it a useful component of dried flower arrangements – could easily be overlooked in the grassland and sand dunes where it grows.

Lesser Burdock
Arctium minus
Alnmouth, July.

Lesser Burdock will be best known for the strong hooked bracts which cause its seedheads to stick to clothing and animal fur alike. A very versatile plant, widespread in the county, it has been used medicinally as well as in the kitchen.

Slender Thistle
Carduus tenuiflorus
Boulmer, June.

Mostly confined to the coastal strip, this attractive thistle with pink flowers is a fairly localised plant in Northumberland.

Spear Thistle
Cirsium vulgare
Holy Island, July.

Said to be the true Scottish thistle, this vigorous plant is extremely widespread and lives up to its name, for the spears on the flowerheads can be very painful if they pierce the skin.

Saw–wort
Serratula tinctoria
Craster, August.

At the northern limit of its British distribution, this is a scarce plant in Northumberland. Superficially resembling knapweeds, to which it is closely related, 'saw–wort' derives from the lobes of its leaves which have a saw–toothed edge.

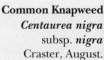

Common Knapweed
Centaurea nigra
subsp. *nigra*
Craster, August.

Also known as hardheads, its knob or 'knap'–like flowerheads give the plant both its common names. It is frequent in numerous habitats stretching from the coast to the uplands of the county.

Cat's ear
Hypochaeris
radicata
Newton Links,
June.

A dandelion
look–alike, cat's
ear is abundant
and the only
member of its
family growing
in the county.
Scale–like
bracts on the
flower–stems
are said to
resemble cats'
ears.

Goat's beard, Jack–go–to–bed–at–noon
Tragopogon pratensis subsp. *minor*
Newton Links, July.

Two names for two different stages in
the plant's life. When in flower, the
distinctive yellow petals, with the green
bracts showing between them, open
fully only on sunny mornings, closing
around mid–day. When in fruit, the
head forms a much more striking
'clock' than a dandelion, enabling the
seeds to be dispersed by the wind.

Dandelion sp.
Taraxacum **sp.**
Alnmouth, May.

A very familiar species even to young children, dandelion is, however, a complex group of species, of which 132 are listed for the British Isles. Like the daisy, it is a much despised and opportunistic plant.

Mouse–ear Hawkweed
Pilosella officinarum
Bamburgh, June.

A widespread relative of the dandelion, it is the shape of the leaf with its hairy surface that is likened to the ear of the rodent.

Fox–and–cubs
Pilosella aurantiaca
Alnmouth, June.

A first cousin to Mouse–ear Hawkweed; unlike that species, this one is not a native, but has escaped from cultivation and occurs in a number of habitats beside coastal links.

Water–plantain
Alisma
plantago–aquatica
Druridge Bay, June.

This native plant of
Northumberland is
also helped in its
distribution by
being planted in
reclamation
schemes. It favours
damp muddy
places either in or
beside shallow
water.

Wildflowers of Coastal Northumberland

Spring Squill
Scilla verna
Cullernose, May.

At its southernmost site on the east coast of Britain, this northern plant likes the short turf above the whinstone of Cullernose Point, where it gives the cropped ground a blue tinge in spring.

Marram
Ammophila arenaria
Newton Links, July.

The first record of this plant in Britain was in Northumberland. Although native to the county, today its abundance, mainly on sand dunes, is accentuated by extensive planting to help stabilise the underlying sand.

Branched Bur–reed
Sparganium erectum
Druridge Bay, June.

Bur–reeds, of which four species grow in the county, get their name from the bur–like heads of the female flowers. They are striking plants of watery or damp areas.

Marsh Helleborine
Epipactis palustris
Holy Island, July.

This member of the orchid family has its Northumberland stronghold in the damp areas of the Snook on Holy Island where thousands of plants may flower. Elsewhere in the county its delicate flowerheads are a much scarcer sight.

Northern Marsh–orchid
Dactylorhiza purpurella
St. Mary's Island, June.

A very abundant orchid in the county, orchids are noted for hybridising with closely related species and may throw up unusual and extra vigorous forms, causing confusion for those trying to identify them.

Early–purple Orchid
Orchis mascula
Warkworth, May.

As the name implies, this is one of the first orchids to flower in spring, and its usually rich purple flowers and blotched narrowish leaves can be found among grassland and sand dunes along the northern half of the county's coastline.

Pyramidal Orchid
Anacamptis pyramidalis
Newton Links, July.

Now mainly confined to coastal dunes, where it is locally common and apparently increasing, its flowerheads vary in colour from pale pink to deep cerise. Its only apparent known pollinator is the Six–Spot Burnet Moth.

73

index

Lesser Sea–spurrey *Spergularia marina*, 4
Lesser Trefoil *Trifolium dubium*, 25
Maidenhair Spleenwort *Asplenium trichomanes*, 1
Marram *Ammophila arenaria*, 69
Marsh Helleborine *Epipactis palustris*, 71
Marsh Woundwort *Stachys palustris*, 48
Meadow Saxifrage *Saxifraga granulata*, 14
Meadow Vetchling *Lathyrus pratensis*, 24
Meadowsweet *Filipendula ulmaria*, 16
Mouse–ear Hawkweed *Pilosella officinarum*, 66
Northern Marsh–orchid *Dactylorhiza purpurella*, 72
Pignut *Conopodium majus*, 33
Pirri–pirri–bur *Acaena novae–zelandiae*, 18
Primrose *Primula vulgaris*, 35
Purple Milk–vetch *Astragalus danicus*, 23
Pyramidal Orchid *Anacamptis pyramidalis*, 73
Ragged–Robin *Lychnis flos–cuculi*, 5
Red Bartsia *Odontites vernus*, 53
Red Campion *Silene dioica*, 6
Red Clover *Trifolium pratense*, 25
Red Valerian *Centranthus ruber*, 55
Rosebay Willowherb *Chamerion augustifolium*, 31
Salad Burnet *Sanguisorba minor*, 18
Saw–wort *Serratula tinctoria*, 63
Scarce Fiddleneck *Amsinckia lycopsoides*, 45
Scarlet Pimpernel *Anagallis arvensis*, 37
Scurvy Grass *Cochlearia officinalis*, 11
Sea Aster *Aster tripolium*, 58
Sea Bindweed *Calystegia soldanella*, 41
Sea Campion *Silene uniflora*, 6
Sea–milkwort *Glaux maritima*, 36
Sea Mouse–ear *Cerastium diffusum*, 4
Sea–purslane *Atriplex portulacoides*, 2
Sea Rocket *Cakile maritima*, 12
Sea Sandwort *Honckenya peploides*, 3
Seaside Centaury *Centaurium littorale*, 39
Silverweed *Potentilla anserina*, 19

Slender St. John's–wort *Hypericum pulchrum*, 30
Slender Thistle *Carduus tenuiflorus*, 61
Small Scabious *Scabiosa columbaria*, 56
Spear Thistle *Cirsium vulgare*, 62
Spring Squill *Scilla verna*, 69
Tansy *Tanacetum vulgare*, 59
Thrift *Armeria maritima*, 37
Tufted Vetch *Vicia cracca*, 22
Viper's–bugloss *Echium vulgare*, 43
Wallflower *Erysimum cheiri*, 10
Water–plantain *Alisma plantago–aquatica*, 68
White Dead–nettle *Lamium album*, 47
White Stonecrop *Sedum album*, 14
Wild Mignonette *Reseda lutea*, 13
Wood Sage *Teucrium scorodonia*, 47
Wild Thyme *Thymus polytrichus*, 48
Yarrow *Achillea millefolium*, 58
Yellow–rattle *Rhinanthus minor*, 53